LIFE

MORE ABUNDANT

LIFE

MORE ABUNDANT

An Owner's Manual

Bill O'Hearn

BookPartners
Wilsonville, Oregon

Other books by Bill O'Hearn:

From the Heart of a Child:
And Other Lessons to Live By

From the Heart of a Lion:
And Other Lessons to Sell By

The Heart of the Matter:
Thoughts to Live By

Library of Congress Cataloging-in-Publication Data
O'Hearn, Bill.
    Life more abundant : an owner's manual / by
Bill O'Hearn.
        p. cm.
        ISBN 1-581-51045-4 (trade paper : alk. paper)
        1. Conduct of life.   1. Self-realization.
    I. Title.
BJ1595.036   1999
170'.44 21--dc21   99-042617

Cover design by Richard Ferguson
Text design by Sheryl Mehary

BookPartners, Inc.
P. O. Box 922
Wilsonville, Oregon 97070

To our seven beautiful grand-children — Amy, Hillary and Nick Philip; Kelsey and Michael Weir; and Connor and Darby O'Hearn. Our fondest wish is that some of the perspectives in this book will find their way into your heart and assist you on your journey through life.

Know we love you and that each of you carries a very special light.

If it sparkles like a diamond,
it must be a gem!
Bill O' Hearn has filled these pages
with one gem after another.
So clear, so simple and so true.
I loved every page.

— Steve Newman

Contents

Acknowledgments

It's tough to write a book. First, there are people who think they know more about how it should be written than you do. The tough part? They are usually right. For the help they gave, over my frequent screams of protest, I thank them. I didn't always enjoy the process — I did enjoy the results.

To the folks at BookPartners: Thorn Bacon, master of paragraph-ripping and literary insight, thank you for the fourth time. Without you, my life would have been easier and my books less. Thank you, Ursula Bacon for your imaginative mind and loving heart in creating the title and cover for this book. Speaking of the cover — Richard Ferguson, you are the master of putting ideas into art form. Thank you for your beautiful work. And thanks as well to Dave Lindstedt, who did the second edit and was a mite easier on me than you-know-who. And to Ginger Marlowe, thanks for your kind heart and insightful answers to my numerous questions during the final edits. Thanks to Sheryl Mehary for putting her unique talents and thoughtfulness into text design and formatting. You are all very special.

To Kathy and Steve Kriesel, two friends who understand grammatical perfection beyond my comprehension, thanks for your unconditional love in the face of my sophomoric mentality. You are great! And to my first "copy readers," Cliff, Greg, Jane, Judy, Lee and Steve, thanks for being so willing to peruse the early manuscript and for encouraging me to keep on recording my thoughts.

To Cliff Canucci, who on several pages tried to play Thorn Bacon — I loved your going the extra mile, even if it did cause me more time in front of the computer. I appreciate you, Cliff, and your beautiful Patty. Thanks as well to Greg Hansen, my stalwart cheerleader. Each manuscript you have critiqued has been done with so much enthusiasm and positive input that I am always reminded how extremely lucky I am to be surrounded by friends like you. Please, always remember how important you are to me and to so many others. Jane LeFors — always there, always encouraging. From my heart to your heart — thanks. Judy Bailey, as always, you were an inspiration. You had already read the manuscript three times by the time I called for your thoughts. You and Cliff have always been there for me. Thank you for being you. And Lee Ross, isn't it wonderful how our friendship has blossomed since those early days, almost ten years ago. You have always been special and both Elizabeth and I love you very much. My thanks to Steve Newman, who decided without solicitation to endorse my book with the most lovingly scripted words any author could hope for.

To the extraordinary folks at the Bend Library reference desk of the Deschutes County Library System, thanks for your enthusiastic pursuit of my requests for verification of certain facts that appear in this book. You are a boon to the entire Central Oregon community.

My appreciation to my friend Al Sizer for his enthusiastic willingness to contact Mark Victor Hansen for an endorsement of this book. You are one very special guy, Al. And to Mark Victor Hansen, thank you once again for your big heart, your generosity, and for all you have accomplished. You are making a difference.

I am deeply grateful for the exceptional friends in my life who brought me to where I am today. I count you among my greatest gifts. Without you, my life would not hold the meaning it has.

No acknowledgment would be complete without mention of my mother, Mary, who is part of everything I have ever accomplished, and Eveard, my very special step-dad, both of whom have now passed on, and my beautiful children and their exceptional spouses — Molly and Eric, Patti and Mark, Julie and Mark and Chip and Joy. You are the underlying motivation for my attempt to put my thoughts on paper.

And finally, thank you, my Elizabeth. Your willingness to read patiently each chapter as it was written and rewritten, and give me your special insight, contributed more than I can tell you to the inspiration needed to stick with my writing. I have thanked you before, but let me say it again: Thank you for being my partner. Thank you for all you do to make our partnership so special. Thank you for being my friend and most of all, thank you for the light you bring to my life. I love you.

All my best ideas
have been stolen
by the ancients.

— Anonymous

Preface

This is a how-to book. Within its pages you will learn how to lead a richer, fuller life. Take to heart those ideas that nudge you. Change of any kind requires commitment and perseverance. If you want more from life, put more right effort into it.

How long does it takes to change? All I know for sure is that I have experienced significant changes in the blink of an eye. And this I can promise you: new, positive perspectives will emerge and bring happiness to you, and in consequence to those around you.

May your time with this book be a journey of *discovery* and *decision* — the discovery of ideas that strike a chord in your heart and in your soul, and the decision to implement those ideas and bring positive change into your life. There is nothing more exciting in the world than reaching for the stars — and discovering *Life More Abundant*.

Let the journey begin.

*All things are possible
to one who believes.*

— St. Bernard of Clairvaux

Chapter 1

Believe in All That
You Are

The purpose of this book is to encourage you to do these two things:

Believe in all that you are.
Become all that you can become.

This chapter is about what you believe.

What a world this would be if each one of us believed in all that we are. Can you imagine the good that would be done, the new things that would be invented, the love that could be shared? This chapter is not about changing the world; it is about changing you — which is the start of changing the world.

We all have hidden talents and unbelievable creativity just sitting there waiting for us to take a quantum leap out of our old selves into our new selves. None of us even comes close to tapping our God-given potential. But if you are to try, you must drop some entrenched ways of thinking and develop a new set of perspectives about who you are. Why is it so tough to do that? What is holding us back? *Past programming!*

A friend of mine is stuck in a life of deprivation because of his past programming. He was born into a family with a demeaning, cruel father. His father repeatedly told him that he would never amount to anything, and that there would never be enough money in his life. Before my friend reached the age of fourteen, his father had knocked him out several times with a fist to the face. Though he possesses all the talent he needs to create the life he wants, he is held back by old beliefs that were literally beaten into him.

It would be easy to argue that it is too difficult to overcome such a brutal background, but I know this man. I know that he has talent far beyond what he thinks he has, and therein lies the problem: *He* doesn't know it, he doesn't believe it.

Will my friend wake up in time? Will he write a new program for his future? I pray that he will and I believe that he will. He is too good not to share with the world the solid gold core of his spirit.

And that goes for all of us. Even with a burning desire to make a difference in the lives of my fellow human beings, I still catch myself limiting my potential. I have no excuse, and neither do you. So let's make a deal. Let's take the blinders off and see ourselves for who we really are.

We enter this world with the innate ability to shape our own destiny, once we make up our mind to do so. We are like lights waiting to be turned on. We all deserve the best, and all you have to do to become all that you can become is to *believe in all that you are.*

*To become all that
you can become,
you must first let go
of who you are.*

— Bill O'Hearn

Chapter 2

Become All That You Can Become

Isn't that why we are here? But if it is, why do most of us go through life settling for less? Remember the phrase used in the last chapter? *Past programming!*

So, if past programming is holding us back, then doesn't it make sense to create some present programming that will allow us to see ourselves in a different light? Is it possible to do this?

In fact, it is done every day. A simple but powerful phrase explains how — to become all that I can become, I must first let go of who I am.

To do this, start with changing the way you think about yourself and your circumstances. Once you believe in all that you are, you have paved the way for future accomplishments.

But just to believe in yourself is not enough. We all know people who understand their potential, at least intellectually, but who are content to rest on past accomplishments. And I would be the last one to sit in judgment of that, since much of my life has been spent that way. But I have had my moments of stretching and stepping out, and when that happened I got a glimpse of the possible.

The catalyst between believing in all that you are and becoming all you can become is *action.* Most of us have a fear of taking action, or don't know how to start. "What if I fail?" we ask, or "What if I don't have what it takes?" or "This is way over my head." and "How can I expect to win when I don't even know how to start?"

How *do* we start? To borrow a perspective from my second book, *From the Heart of a Lion,* "With a big enough *why,* the *how* doesn't matter."

Recently I was introduced to an interesting insight that went something like this:

> *When you come to the edge of all the light you have, and must take a step into the darkness of the unknown, believe that one of two things will happen to you. Either there will be something solid to stand on, or you will be taught to fly.*

If you decide to take the path of becoming all that you can become, I believe you will be shown the way. Remember it is not a destination you are seeking. It is a process — the evolution of your spirit.

Happy flying.

Faith is to believe
what you do not yet see;
the reward for this faith
is to see what you believe.

— St. Augustine

Chapter 3

Believe in Unlimited Possibilities

We all have limits on our thinking; nevertheless, I ask you to dream without limits. To live your life fully on earth, it is important to remove barriers to what is possible. What would happen in your life if you suddenly gained new insights? What would you change? Would relationships flourish? Would your financial life prosper, your physical self become stronger? Would your heart be filled with joy? The answer to these questions is a resounding *yes* — if you decide that is what you want. Always remember, anything you decide *irrevocably* that you can do, you can do. Period.

In 1888, the first land speed record was set at 39.2 miles per hour. Then in 1965, Craig Breedlove hurtled past 600 miles per hour. Since that time scientists insisted that it was impossible to break the 700 miles per hour sound barrier on land. However, in 1997 along came Royal Air Force Captain Andy Green, who didn't accept the impossible. He broke the sound barrier in Black Rock Desert in Nevada with a speed of 714.1 miles per hour, with a 10-ton roadster named Thrust, powered by two Rolls-Royce jet engines. A few weeks later he broke the barrier again with an average speed of 763 miles per hour that left the experts looking for something else to put a limit on.

But let us get closer to home. In my book, *From the Heart of a Lion,* I tell the story of an autumn day forty-three years ago. On that day, which started out like any other, I decided in a flash of insight that I could, after four years of failing in the life insurance business, sell as much insurance in one year as I had in the previous four years. I could go from the bottom of the heap to become one of the top 2 percent of all producers in the world. I could rocket from failure to success. I could make the impossible possible.

I had no idea how to accomplish this. I only knew my decision was *irrevocable.* There would be no trying, there would be only doing.

Then in January of that big goal year, I did one very important thing. While attending a meeting of about forty of my peers from our insurance company, I announced in front of all of them that I was going to do something no one in our company had ever done — sell a million dollars of insurance in one year. Announcing my intentions to my colleagues and friends sealed my fate. Now, my ego had too much on the line to fail. I knew what I had to do, and I did it.

By the end of the year I had sold just over one million dollars worth of insurance. That one flash of insight into what was possible changed my whole world, and the world of my family, forever.

Why not seek a flash of your own? Discard the old ways of thinking that aren't serving you well and seek to make the impossible possible. I guarantee you'll find excitement and fun, and your life can be changed forever.

What is beyond
a life of success?
A life of meaning!

— Bill O'Hearn

Chapter 4

Understand Success

Oh, how we strive for success, all the while misunderstanding what it really is. Where did all our striving for success originate? Some would attribute it to the Protestant work ethic. Others might say it is just part of being human. Regardless of its source, "Going for the Gold" is a way of life for many of us. For most, the "Gold" is defined as money, power, fancy cars, big houses and moving up through the ranks.

Sooner or later, trophies lose their luster and the glory begins to fade. In its place, we find midlife crises and burnout — common maladies for those who have been on the success treadmill for years.

When it happened to me, about thirty years ago, I remember asking myself, "What do I really want to do when I grow up?" But I wasn't ready to stop striving.

And although I knew there was more to life, I couldn't figure it out, so I bought a bigger car, and built a bigger house.

I was having more fun than almost anyone I knew, but my striving to scale the pinnacle of success continued for many, many years — along with my feeling that something was missing. Then, gradually, for reasons unclear to me (maybe the natural evolution of my soul), I began to seek another direction. I started to work on developing myself as a person. Eventually, I realized that success isn't gained by what I do. True success comes from who I am.

I should have been asking the question, "Who do I really want to be when I grow up?"

When I changed my focus, material wealth became less important. In fact, I came close to bankruptcy twice, yet I seemed more fulfilled. Not completely fulfilled by any means, but I knew I was on the path. I'm not there yet, but I am moving along. And I finally came to the realization that the path is what is important, not the final destination.

A message that held great meaning for me appeared in Carlos Casteneda's book, *The Teachings of Don Juan: A Yaqui Way of Knowledge*. Don Juan and Carlos were discussing various paths in life. Don Juan says:

> *"My benefactor told me about it once when I was young, but my blood was too*

*vigorous for me to understand it. Now I
do understand it. I will tell you what it is:
Does this path have a heart? All paths
are the same: they lead nowhere. They
are paths going through the bush or into
the bush. In my own life I could say I
have traversed long, long paths, but I am
not anywhere. My benefactor's question
has meaning now. Does this path have a
heart? If it does, the path is good; if it
doesn't it is of no use. Both paths lead
nowhere; but one has a heart, the other
doesn't. One makes for a joyful journey;
as long as you follow it, you are one with
it. The other will make you curse your
life. One makes you strong; the other
weakens you."*

It is important for you that your path has a
heart. Real success comes from your success as
a human being. Success is being aware of
growing in all areas of life — the mental,
physical, social, financial, relational, and espe-
cially the spiritual. Perhaps growing in all the
other areas is what the spiritual is all about.

I have a wood carving of a coat of arms
hanging on the wall of my office. At the bottom
of the plaque, carved in Gaelic to celebrate my
Irish background, are these words: *Happiness is
the pursuit of excellence.*

If you are on the path of pursuing excellence in all areas of your life — believing in all that you are and striving to become all that you can be — then you are successful. Life is not about perfection; it is about progress.

Good luck to you, and great progress.

Finally, we learn that
if we are to celebrate,
it must be for today alone.
This moment —
whatever it brings —
is the gift.
Our celebration of today
creates the laugh lines
on the face of tomorrow.

— Anonymous

Chapter 5

Live in the Present

How much precious time is spent wallowing in the past? Why this tremendous preoccupation with something we can do nothing about? Don't we realize that any time spent in the past negates the present moment? Everyone has experienced failures and successes, tribulations and triumphs, but some people spend a great part of their lives rehashing the bad stuff, or reliving past glories.

I can't emphasize strongly enough the importance of letting the past go — the good, the bad and the ugly — and living for the present moment. Sometimes it seems that very few of us, including me, take time to appreciate that *now* is all there really is. We can dream about the future, agonize over what might have been, or regret what was, but change can happen only in the here and now.

However, the past is important for one reason: it contains the experiences that lead us to wisdom. One bit of wisdom I gained while watching my first wife, Gloria, lose her battle with Alzheimer's, came as the result of my decision not to allow two lives to be destroyed by this tragic disease. As this beautiful fifty-one-year-old woman gradually deteriorated over the last twelve years of her life into a person none of us knew, I easily could have piled up regrets for everything I did or didn't do during the first thirty-two years of our marriage. I could have elected to give up the joy of living my life, as Gloria became more childlike.

Instead, I chose to give thanks for our four beautiful children, our grandchildren, and our friends. I consciously decided to celebrate life. I chose to live in the present in a state of caring, giving Gloria love in place of impatience, smiles and songs instead of tears, and acceptance of what was instead of frustration for what might have been. I can now look back and realize that this adversity was given to me as a tool for future growth. The experience wasn't good, but it was purposeful. And I discovered the importance of taking time in the present, regardless of circumstances, to create my attitudes for the future.

Some food for thought: Every single day from now on, regardless of your circumstances, attempt to be aware of your blessings and say a heartfelt thank you to your God for being fully alive, fully in the present. Then *live* in that present! You'll be glad you did, and the universe will be a better place because of you.

*Your work
is to discover your work,
and then,
with all your heart,
to give yourself to it.*

— Buddha

Chapter 6

Write Your Own Music, Dance Your Own Dance

How many times in your life have you found yourself marching to someone else's drum? More often than you'd care to admit? It seems like we are forever being pulled and pushed by the demands of family, job and community. Sometimes even your own internal drummer strikes up a compelling beat and you find yourself doing something you *think* you should do though you're not even sure it is the right thing to do. Maybe it is a meeting or a party that you really have no desire to attend, but you go for the sake of appearance. Have you been there? Sure you have. We all have.

Is it time to stop dancing to someone else's music? You'll have to answer that question for yourself, but for me the answer is, *absolutely and definitely yes!* Why am I so emphatic? Because I have seen too many people

~ *23* ~

with beautiful spirit and talent spend their days building someone else's dream.

I am reminded of the story of a young man who applied for a sales job with a small firm owned by a man of vision, an entrepreneur with big plans. In the process of the job interview, the owner took the young man out to the country to show him an unbelievably stunning estate. The grounds were impeccably manicured. There was a handsome stable and paddock for the horses. An impressive mansion overlooked a beautiful lake and at the dock sat a regal-looking yacht. This place had everything!

The business owner put his arm around the shoulder of the young man and with a sweeping gesture toward all they surveyed, said, "Look at this beautiful estate. If you come to work for me and pay the price, keep your eye on the ball, work long hours and keep your nose to the grindstone, then someday all this will be *mine.*"

Therein lies the point of this chapter. If you don't write your own music and choreograph your own life, you'll be singing someone else's song and dancing someone else's dance. You'll be making someone else's dream come true.

You needn't be an entrepreneur or in business for yourself, if that is not your inclination. But you must work at something that draws out your special spirit and affords the opportunity to make your own dreams come true.

You have more talent and more potential than you can ever comprehend. But if you will begin to visualize what might be possible, using your creative imagination to script your own life, to *write your own music and dance your own dance,* all kinds of opportunities will open up. Your entire existence will take on new meaning. I hope you go for it. You'll be glad you did.

Simplicity is a significant intellectual achievement.

— Anonymous

Chapter 7

Keep It Simple

During a period in my insurance sales career that now seems like a hundred years ago, KISS was a popular acronym for "keep it simple, stupid." I never liked the "stupid" part and related to the KISS principle more when my friend and colleague Tom Wolff , past president of the National Association of Life Underwriters, suggested that we "keep it simple and sincere."

Even though I bought in to the idea, it took me years to put the principle into action. I was too busy showing how smart I was. I took uncomplicated insurance concepts and turned them into pages of meaningless boilerplate. Then I placed the pages in a fancy notebook and presented them to prospective clients. I was certain they would be impressed with me. I kept telling them how to make a clock when all they wanted to know was what time it was. I ended up calling this phase my "complicated sophistication" period.

Eventually I grasped the principle of mature simplicity, much to the relief of my prospects — who more often than not became my clients. I discovered that initially they were more interested in how much I cared than in how much I knew.

As I reflect on life, I see evidence that far too many of us complicate matters beyond reason. We put on airs for the benefit of ego and in the process we don't allow beautiful, simple spirit to shine through.

Do I always keep it (life) simple and sincere? No. Is it possible to keep life simple and sincere? Yes. It is not only possible, but essential. Simplicity is my goal. With simplicity comes awareness — which is key to accomplishment.

When we keep life simple we erase greed, restore laughter, gain a childlike heart, give more love, receive more love, and the list simply goes on and on.

Take a look inside yourself. Do a little assessment to determine where you are on your path. Then make an absolute commitment to your spirit to KISS — *keep it simple and sincere.*

Intuition —
the insight of spirit.

— Bill O'Hearn

Chapter 8

Listen to Your Intuition

Even though I have advocated for years that the power to choose is the greatest gift we have been given, I sometimes wonder whether the most important gift isn't actually the gift of intuition — a gift which is, unfortunately, all too often overlooked or ignored.

In her book, *The Game of Life and How to Play It,* Florence Scovil Shinn says, "Prayer is you telephoning God. Intuition is God telephoning you." I agree. But if our intuition is God-driven, or God-given, why do we so often refuse to listen?

Perhaps because we live in a predominately left-brained, logical world, something as subjective as feelings is easy to dismiss as fantasy, or an impractical daydream. Too often, we ignore intuition. The net result of letting intuition go is that we let go of what might be.

We let go of possibilities for a more enlightened and guided life.

Assuming that you wish to expand your life possibilities, what can you do? Start by praying for awareness. Ask your Creator, your guide, or your guardian angel to expand your thinking so that when intuition looks in on you, you pay attention.

Then ask for the courage to *act*. It is one thing to *feel* that you should do something, but quite another thing to act on that feeling.

Is it always right to act on feelings? I don't know. But permit me to advance a theory. If you will listen — on purpose and with great awareness — to your intuition, it can lead you on a more enlightened path. It can put you in touch with a part of yourself that speaks for your greatest good, and for the greatest good of all. If you accept your intuition as a gift, give thanks for the blessing, and follow your feelings, your life will take on new and exciting dimensions.

To be wronged is nothing
unless you continue to
remember it.

— Confucius

Chapter 9

Always Forgive

A friend of ours, Mary Manin Morrissey, founder and senior minister of the Living Enrichment Center in Wilsonville, Oregon, and author of *Building Your Field of Dreams,* delivered a sermon one Sunday in which she spoke about the biology of hope. That sermon set me to wondering if the biology of our body is affected by practicing forgiveness.

A couple of close friends of mine went through a traumatic experience in their business when someone in whom they had complete trust embezzled a large sum of money. The loss of money was significant, but even more devastating was the sense of betrayal they suffered. Within a few days my friends had to make an important choice. Could they find it in their hearts to forgive this trespass of spirit and soul? Or would they fall into the familiar trap of smoldering in anger?

They were facing a potentially life-changing decision. The money was gone, never to be replaced, and their friend would be dealt with by the authorities — that part was out of their hands. What now? Would their hearts be filled with forgiveness, or with hatred and bitter-ness?

They chose forgiveness. Had they chosen hatred, their bodies would have been powerfully dosed with negative emotion. I am convinced, and many well-known authorities such as Deepak Chopra, Joan Borysenko, Larry Dossey and Bernie Seigel agree, that our thoughts have the power to influence change in cellular structure. In other words, our thoughts influence the biology of our bodies.

If our thoughts affect our bodies, does it not follow that those fearful thoughts, hateful thoughts, jealous thoughts and angry thoughts should be removed from our lives?

Could my friends have simply shrugged their shoulders as though nothing had happened? No. Something significant had happened, and it had happened to them. Without an active decision-making process, the danger of default thinking might have taken over. Fortunately, my friends understood their ability — and their responsibility — to choose and they understood that the universe sometimes acts in strange ways. They decided to forgive and to put the circumstance behind them, and, in the process, they chose to give their bodies a better chance for health.

I hope you will pause for a moment and think about the circumstances in your life. Are there any past situations in which forgiveness has not yet been granted? If there are, remember to *always forgive*. Your body and your spirit will appreciate your proactive, healthy decision.

*To be aware of
who you want to be
is the beginning
of the path.*

— Bill O'Hearn

Chapter 10

Practice Awareness

For many years, I have embraced the concept of personal growth as a vital, ongoing process. I have been setting goals for personal improvement for so long now that I should qualify as the guru of goal-setting. The only challenge to that title might be, "How long have you been setting the *right* goals?"

When I read the goals I set during the past twenty-five years, I realize they are significantly different from the goals I set before. My initial goals had to do with money and the things money could buy. Now, as I look back, I realize that I gained those outward symbols of success because I was constantly *aware* of what I wanted.

As the years went by, I began to realize that true happiness was going to come to me only as a result of growing in all areas of my life — not just in the financial portion of my life.

So I decided that I wanted to become a more patient person. In particular, I wanted to show more love and patience to my wife Gloria (who has since passed on) and to my children. In the early years, patience was not a redeeming quality of mine. And so began the era of goal-setting for the whole person — my attempt to become the best human being I could be. But the results didn't come as readily as they had with the material goals, and I wasn't exactly sure why.

Eventually, I realized that my personal growth goals had not taken over my consciousness as my money and ego goals had. I wasn't constantly aware of being more caring, more loving, more patient, or more understanding. So I decided to try and practice *constant awareness* in these areas.

Even though I have gradually shifted my awareness over the years, I have never, not once in my life, spent as much thought and energy on becoming the person I want to be as I spent on gaining the materially good things in life. But because I am now more aware, on a fairly consistent basis, of my goals as a whole person, I'm further along the path than if I had just wandered around hoping I would get better.

So, let me urge you to have goals about the kind of person you want to be, and then moment by moment, as much as it is possible, be aware of those goals. One thing is bound to happen if you do: You will change and you will be different tomorrow than you are today. And because of that, your world will be better.

*There is no quality
I would rather have,
or be thought to have,
than gratitude.
It is not only
the greatest virtue,
it is the mother
of all the rest.*

— Cicero

Chapter 11

Live with Gratitude

If you wish to have a fulfilling life, you absolutely must be grateful for everything. Your reaction to this statement might be one of skepticism. How can one possibly be grateful for everything? Full-scale gratitude is not only possible, it's also probable. If you adopt the perspective that no matter what happens — a car accident, sickness, divorce or even the death of a loved one — within every life experience lies a lesson that will help you on your path to being a fully evolved human spirit.

Which brings us to the next red flag. Is it possible for anyone to become a fully evolved human spirit? Well, of course it is possible. Jesus did it. And those of other faiths might suggest that their figurehead of God is a fully evolved human spirit. But what about you and me? My present perspective is that the vast majority of human beings will not completely evolve spiritually while in the earth dimension. When we leave this earth, we are no longer human beings — unless reincarnation is part of the spirit's existence. But even with reincarnation, it seems to me that we are still not going to make it in this dimension. My long-term perspective, on the other hand, is that, yes, we will all become evolved spirits — eventually.

Which brings me back to gratitude. The mere possibility that you and I will eventually evolve gives us enough reason to live in a state of perpetual gratitude.

"So," you might ask, "if we will evolve eventually, why go to the trouble of trying to walk the path to enlightenment?" My guess is that there is continuing education after death, which means that the more we evolve here on earth, the more quickly we become one with our Creator.

I'm not addressing the subject of heaven and hell. You will have to work that out for yourself.

Here's a story that epitomizes living with gratitude:

A group of Buddhist students sat listening to the Master. Each asked the question, "How many lifetimes will I experience before I see God?" and the Master answered each with, "two lifetimes," "five lifetimes," and so on. When the star student asked "How many lifetimes?" the Master answered, "A million lifetimes."

The other students were shocked. The most outstanding student had to experience a million lifetimes. The students felt bad for their friend. A bit later they noticed that he was missing. They went looking for him and found him outside, dancing.

"How can you be dancing and singing after what you have just been told?" they asked.

The star student answered, "Don't you see? Our Master told me that I am going to see God."

༺❦༻

So, in your own life, be thankful. Be filled with gratitude for everything. Remember, even though you may not evolve completely here on earth, your reason for being here is to try. Eventually, you will be rewarded.

༺❦༻

*Courage and perseverance
have a magical talisman,
before which difficulties
and obstacles
vanish into air.*

— John Quincy Adams

Chapter 12

Live with Boundless Courage

When I think of boundless courage, the first thing that comes to mind is standing tall in the face of great danger such as fighting a war, or risking your life to save someone from a fire. Many other examples come to mind that suggest a level of valor to which few of us will be called.

However, there is a courage that matches, and I believe exceeds, even great acts of heroism. This brand of courage will not result in being awarded the Congressional Medal of Honor. In fact, it may never even come to light. I'm referring to the courage of living life as though boundaries do not exist; living life not because of circumstances, but rather, in spite of circumstances

This is epitomized in the life of a young man named Ron Heagy. In March of 1980 Ron was a senior at Central Linn High School located near his hometown of Brownsville, Oregon. He was three months away from graduating and the following school year a football scholarship awaited him at Oregon State University. After graduation from college, he was sure that an NFL career would follow.

Spring break was coming, and Ron looked forward to a visit to Southern California to learn to surf and get some time in the sun with friends. As it turned out, he begrudgingly had to take Mike, his thirteen-year-old brother, with him. Ron didn't know his life was about to be changed forever.

On their second day at Huntington Beach, the waves were too flat for surfing, so Ron and Mike and their friend Justin decided to lay on the beach and soak up some rays.

Shortly, Ron became restless and decided a dip in the beautiful Pacific was in order. The water felt really chilly, but while he was considering whether to dip or not to dip, he spotted a wave beginning to crest. Without hesitation, he ran toward it and dove into the breaker. Hidden from sight was a sandbar that Ron crashed into headfirst. He experienced an excruciating pain in his neck.

As fortune would have it Mike had raised up and saw his brother take the plunge. He saw Ron's body flip in a quick somersault and then disappear. Mike realized something was wrong and immediately ran into the surf. The next several minutes contained a miracle, in which an incredibly brave 120-pound thirteen-year-old managed to get his helpless 195-pound brother out of fifteen feet of treacherous water.

To get the full impact of the moment, you need to read Ron's book, authored by him with Donita Dyer, entitled *Life is an Attitude.* But the net result of this catastrophic accident is that Ron is quadriplegic.

Now in his thirties, Ron travels across the country sharing his incredible message about the power of positive thinking. I had the good fortune of hearing Ron talk in 1997. His message is one we all need to hear, a story of triumph over tragedy.

A most extraordinary example of his courage is seen in the beautiful paintings he creates by holding a paintbrush between his teeth. Put Ron's book on your must-read list. *(For more information about Ron and his dramatic story, look in the back of this book.)*

Boundless courage like Ron's requires an understanding of one's purpose and a commitment to fulfill that purpose.

But how do you discover your purpose, and how do you find the courage to pursue your purpose? I have been asking myself these questions for a long, long time. My best guess is this: You must develop openness and listen to the universe. Does it have a plan for you? Does God have a plan for you?

It takes courage to be trusting. It takes courage to believe that you can ask and that you will receive. It takes courage to believe that there are no coincidences and once we make the effort to follow our calling, it takes courage to trust that everything is working out as it should. It takes courage to follow your heart instead of your head.

Boundless courage is stepping off the treadmill, stepping outside the comfort zone, pursuing what you would really like to do.

If you learn to listen to your heart — and with your heart — you will be given boundless courage to pursue your purpose, your path, your reason for being here. And life will be full.

*Through balance
you achieve peace.
Through peace
you achieve insight.
Through insight
you achieve wisdom.
Be balanced —
and be wise.*

— Bill O'Hearn

Chapter 13

Balance Your Week

A prevalent thought in the workplace today is, "I'm moving too fast. I've got to slow down and get some *balance* in my life." When I encountered these thoughts from time to time over the past forty-plus years, getting balance in my life seemed like an overwhelming project — until I did something in my life insurance career that led to a positive change.

After I had finally broken through the failure barrier and was on my way to conventional success, I found myself running so hard that at times my heart hurt. This led to a call to the doctor, who admonished me to slow down. He gave me some little red pills to take when I found myself going too fast — which was all the time. I put the pills in the glove compartment of

my car and refused to take any, believing that I
could figure out a better way.

The realization that I was all work and not
much play led me to a life changing and
possibly lifesaving decision. I decided to take
every Thursday off, *if* I could do a week's work
by Wednesday night. I wanted to play on
Thursdays, Saturdays and Sundays, so I had to
become more effective in my time management.
And I did. In the process, I brought some
balance into my life. As the years passed I began
to realize that there was more to balance in life
than simply working four days and taking three
days off. My perspective expanded to include
balance in all areas of my life.

Recently, I developed another perspective
that adds to my balance. Each and every day for
the rest of my life, I have promised myself to do
these two specific things:

- Give thanks for all the blessings in my life,
  my wife Elizabeth, my children and their
  spouses, my grandchildren, my mother and
  stepdad who have passed on, my health, our
  beautiful home, all our friends, all the love in
  my life and on and on and on.

- Find a special time each and every day just
  for enjoyment, whether it's practicing on the
  golf range or walking in nature, sitting down

with a good book, or possibly all of the above — anything that makes my heart sing. That is my promise to myself.

I could have titled this chapter "Balance Your Day," but if you're like me, you're going to struggle to get the big picture down to one week at a time. If you can do that, eventually you can bring joy into your life on a daily basis. You may not have a job or career that will allow you to work four days and play three; nevertheless, if you work on balance within the time you have, I guarantee your whole life will fill with happiness.

*Only by sharing your light
can you bring brightness
to your world.*

— Bill O'Hearn

Chapter 14

Let Your Light Shine

Let your light shine.

"What light?" you ask.

The light that was given you when you were born.

Did you know there is a light that shines brightly within all of us, but sometimes not very brightly without? This light is *spirit,* your spirit.

How is it possible that we have this light and yet no one can see it? Well, the truth is that we do see shining lights but we haven't given credit to spirit. Past and present examples of shining lights are Michelangelo, Mother Teresa, Einstein, Linus Pauling, Katherine Hepburn, Gandhi, Florence Nightingale, Rogers and Hammerstein, Spencer Tracy, Princess Diana, James Stewart, Ella Fitzgerald, Nat King Cole,

Madame Curie, Bruce Springsteen — even Elvis. Some might say, especially Elvis.

"But these are the exceptions," you say. No, they are the proof. Most of us simply haven't let our light shine. But, trust me, your light is there waiting to be turned on.

If it is there, why has no one ever seen it? You could ask the same question about the light that shines outside your body — your aura. Not many years ago, few believed that light surrounds us. But now it can be photographed using a technique called Kirlian photography.

If it is possible for us to have an outer light, why not an inner light? Proof of the inner light comes in many more ways than through the talents of famous people. I believe it shows itself through all kinds of people in all kinds of situations.

The firm of Norman Building and Design recently built a new home for Elizabeth and me. The caring and the talent of those involved in the project can be sensed as well as seen. Their special lights, individually and combined, gave us a home instead of a house.

Each one of us possesses a special light that we can shine at any time, if we so choose. How? As simply as smiling at a stranger, giving with no expectations of receiving, offering unconditional love, or taking that special talent that is within us and sharing it with the world.

Yes, the light of spirit is definitely in you. Your mission, should you decide to accept it, is to *let your light shine.*

Adversity is unavoidable.
Suffering is optional.

— Anonymous

Chapter 15

Handle Your Circumstances

You don't have to look far to find examples of people not handling their circumstances. Circumstances handle them instead. Go for a drive sometime. Have you ever let bad drivers or other traffic problems bother you? But it isn't just traffic. Your whole life is composed of circumstances. Some may be unpleasant, such as an angry spouse or an errant child, a bad golf shot, a divorce, financial problems, poor health or getting fired.

Circumstances can also be rosy. You may have a loving spouse, land a dream job, be blessed with a baby, receive a clean bill of health, or witness a beautiful sunset.

You will always be surrounded by circumstances — some are to your liking, some are not. Sooner or later

you have to make up your mind about how to
react to circumstances. You might say, "It
depends upon the circumstance you are talking
about." I would reply that it doesn't make any
difference — in order to lead a happy, fulfilling
life, you must decide in advance how to react to
circumstances.

If you don't prepare your attitude before
the fact, then circumstances will automatically
control your life, and you will end up with
unhappiness during your time here on earth. It
took me years to learn this concept, through a
variety of circumstances ranging from minor to
major and from good to bad.

Handling your circumstances is similar to
the power to choose. For a broader discussion of
the power to choose, see my first book, *From the
Heart of a Child.* However, the perspective
described herein is about circumstances that
happen to you, not circumstances you decide to
create.

But sometimes, circumstances are so
sudden and so overwhelming that we may not
have had time to consider how to react. The
unexpected death of a loved one, for instance, is
such a circumstance. Then we are forced to
make moment-to-moment decisions.

In 1993, Dick, a widower friend of mine,
married Pat, a widow who was not only a special
human being, but also a very talented artist.

They traveled far and wide and visited Jackson Hole, Wyoming, during the summer so Pat could perfect her painting technique in a class offered there. They lived in the same neighborhood as Elizabeth and I and we saw them occasionally, sometimes at exhibits of Pat's works. They were very much in love and they led a beautiful life. They were perfect for each other.

But during an extended trip to Africa, Dick became ill and was hospitalized immediately upon their return. He was determined to get well, but it was more than his body could handle. Dick passed away after six weeks in intensive care, and Pat was devastated. After five years of bliss, she was left alone for the second time in her life.

I talked with Pat on the phone and asked if she would consider picking up her paintbrush to soothe her sorrow. But for Pat, the burden of losing Dick was too great to even consider painting. I felt that Dick would not have wanted her to stop painting, even for a while, so I urged her to just think about it.

Pat was faced with the decision to remain immobilized or to somehow take action. A short time later, a mutual friend told me that Pat had started painting again — in spite of her sad circumstances. In visiting with Pat, a little over a year later, she related to me how she had made the decision to create beauty both through her paintings of flowers and by planting and growing a wonderful garden.

Pat could have prolonged her sadness, but she elected to take action. Pat *handled* her circumstances, and I'm sure Dick is looking down and smiling.

The next time you face your own circumstance, remember that you can choose how to react to it. Take control of your life for your own best interest. Your life will be enhanced. And maybe, just maybe, after a while, with practice, you will own this simple perspective: *Circumstances don't count!*

All we are is the result
of what we have thought.

— Buddha

Chapter 16

Monitor Your Thoughts

Monitor your thoughts. Why? Because the quality of your life depends on it. Thoughts run through your mind (and often out of your mouth) at an incredible rate of speed. In doing research for my Alpha Learning Institute seminars I discovered that the average person talks at a speed of about one hundred fifty to two hundred fifty words per minute. But I also discovered that words running through our minds travel at the rate of eight hundred to fourteen hundred words per minute. This is good news if those words and the thoughts behind them are positive. However, psychologists have estimated that 85 percent of our mental images are negative. That does not mean good conversation with others or with ourselves.

I decided a long time ago that I would make a conscious effort to be aware of my thoughts. I didn't decide this arbitrarily, but only after being exposed to an array of evidence that *as our thoughts go — so goes our life.*

Years ago, I heard the story of a woman who just *knew* she was going to get cancer. I can't remember if there was a family history or some other rationale for her thoughts, but she was adamant. Not only was she convinced that she was going to get cancer, but she also knew where it would appear. It took years, but her thoughts finally won and she was diagnosed with breast cancer at the exact spot she had predetermined. This story made an impact on me and I made a mental note to watch what I thought and said.

Then, in my research into human potential, I began to see evidence that positive mental imaging and silent or spoken words can positively affect the health of the body. I became convinced that if I wanted good health, and what I thought about had a significant impact on my health, I had better think good thoughts.

Even today it is sometimes easy to slide into less-than-positive thoughts, but most of the time I'm sufficiently aware to pull the switch on the negative and replace it with a positive.

Can you imagine the quality of life of a person who nurtures hate and resentment? Can you imagine the life of the people around that person? Not a beneficial experience for anybody.

Health is vital to having a greater life. But, what about the other areas of your life — financial, relational, spiritual and so on? Let go of the bad and nurture the good in every area of your life.

A good friend of mine, Pat Kaufmann, has a great comeback when he hears someone utter a negative statement. Pat merely says, with a gentle smile and a kind of soft inquisitiveness, "Is that what you want?"

Let me ask you this: Is what you think about most of the time what you really want in your life? If it is, congratulations. If not, ask yourself, *"Is that what I want?"*

No one can predict to what
heights you can soar.
Even you will not know
until you spread your wings.

— Anonymous

Chapter 17

Stretch Yourself

This is not a chapter about physical exercise. When I say, "stretch yourself," I'm talking about those moments when you have the opportunity to go beyond your point of comfort and to put yourself on the front line.

During my career in the life insurance industry, the front lines were easy to find — as easy as picking up a phone. Every time I even thought about calling a stranger on the phone to ask for an appointment, I received a message from my ego that said, "Don't take the chance of getting rejected." Yet, to survive, I had to. Those who don't make it in a sales career are those who can't bring themselves to stretch.

How about you? Are there areas in your life where some stretch of imagination or courage is required to accomplish certain things? If you're human, there are. Are you reluctant to strike up a conversation with a stranger, or ask directions, or stand in front of a group and make a speech? Each one of us has areas in our lives that are subject to the fragile nature of the ego. And yet, to experience life at its best, we *must* go beyond the comfortable if we are to realize even a small part of what our life can be.

I don't know why God made us this way. Wouldn't it be more fun if we stretched naturally and didn't even recognize such a thing as a comfort zone?

All the success I have experienced has required me to go beyond what I really wanted to do — or not do. Sometimes I stretched. Sometimes I didn't. If you pinned me down, I would have to admit that the times I didn't stretch far outnumbered the times I did.

Once I had the opportunity to buy 640 acres of beautiful Central Oregon property that I had admired for years. I talked to the owner a couple of times and we finally agreed to a tentative price. I could raise the money by selling twenty-acre plots to friends who loved this part of Oregon. If I could sell the twenty plots at twenty-five thousand dollars apiece I would raise all the money I needed and still have 240 acres for my own ranch — free and clear. As it turned out, the very first person I talked to said yes. I was confident I could easily find nineteen more willing buyers.

Then my logical mind decided to get involved — enough of this dreaming stuff. I started asking myself questions like, "How will people get to their land without roads?" and "Who am I to take on a project that involves so many things I know nothing about?" Finally, the enormity of the task overwhelmed me and I gave up the dream of owning the ranch. I didn't go to the next step; brainstorming with someone experienced in land development. I had the chance to fulfill a dream, but I couldn't bring myself to do something I knew nothing about. It was too much of a stretch.

A knowledgeable developer eventually bought the property, and today there are multitudes of beautiful homes there, many of them worth more than the original price for the entire 640 acres.

જજ

The moral of the story is, think big, and follow through. The next time you are faced with an opportunity to grow, adding new dimension to your life, make up your mind to *stretch yourself.* It won't always be comfortable, but it will be worth it. Guaranteed.

જજ

You are too great for small dreams.

— Bill O'Hearn

Chapter 18

Dream Big Dreams

Dream big dreams.

Easy to say, not easy to do. And yet, creating and dreaming big dreams is the secret to living a happy, exciting and fulfilling life. As the saying goes, if you don't have a dream, you can't have a dream come true.

This chapter is about encouraging you to make dreams, *really big dreams,* a part of your everyday life.

Let me tell you about a dream I had a long time ago. Sometime in the early 1950s, I dreamed of owning a home that looked as though it had been around for a hundred years, but a hundred years later would still look the same. It would be a house of substance. I wanted it to look like a house that could have been owned by a president of the United States. This really was a wild dream. I went so far as to pick up a magazine that showed all the houses of our past presidents. And as I looked at them I said to myself, "Yes, that's what I want."

Well, at the time, Gloria and I were just starting our family. Figuring out how to pay the utility bill on time each month was about as much as I could handle. But I kept my big dream in the back of my mind. By the late 1950s, I was going from failure to success in my insurance business, and we decided to build a home. Not the home I had visualized, but a nice two-story, four bedroom, two-and-a-half-bathroom Cape Cod-style home. It was comfortable, located in a great neighborhood, and a good place to raise our children.

Life was good, but the dream persisted. I didn't think about it all the time, but every now and then I refined the details in my mind. Then, in the mid-1960s we had a chance to buy a big lot down the street from us — half an acre, with wilderness in back that would never be developed. It would be a good investment no matter what.

Finally, in 1969, the big dream said NOW. We met with an architect and I described my vision. He used his imagination but designed something that bore no resemblance to what I had in mind.

He tried twice more, and finally, exasperated, he said to me, "The trouble with you, Bill, is that you have a champagne appetite and a beer income." We ended the relationship then and there — even though he had hit the nail on the head.

I began to search through architectural magazines, *Sunset* magazine and other periodicals, until I found a picture of a beautiful French country home that had the flavor and the beauty I was looking for. We decided to take the picture to Frank Merrill, a friend who had designed the home we were living in. I told him what we had experienced with the architect, including the wisecrack. He studied the picture, asked some in-depth questions and finally said, "I believe we can make it happen." Those words were the beginning of a dream come true.

The process was a long one, but several serendipitous events added to the home's beauty. A historic tavern in downtown Albany, Oregon — the Lady Gay Saloon — had been razed and we were able to buy its 40,000 used bricks. Our home would honor a part of Albany's history.

Months into construction, we were introduced to a well-known landscape designer. The circular driveway was near completion and the entrance to the house was in its final stages. She placed some of the used brick around the driveway and added a big aggregate concrete front porch surrounded by more of the used brick plus a beautiful water fountain. What a difference this made!

The result, many months later, was a 5,000-square-foot home with two stories and a full basement, five bedrooms, four full baths, and a beautiful interior filled with gorgeous antiques — a president's home if ever I saw one. And guess what, I was *president* — of a publicly held insurance company. Coincidence?

My point is not to brag about a house I once owned. My hope is to encourage you to dream a big dream, one that seems beyond your immediate grasp.

Spend quality time creating that dream in your imagination. You may pray, meditate or visualize, but in order to make it happen, you must invest the time necessary to explore what is possible.

Then hold on to it, play it over and over in your mind, and someday you may have a chance to have your dream come true.

No matter how small
or unimportant
what we are doing
may seem,
if we do it well
it may soon become
the step that will lead us
to better things.

— Channing Pollock

Chapter 19

Clean the Garage

Yuck! I can think of a thousand things I'd rather do than clean the garage. You too? The same applies to the metaphorical "garage" that represents all those things in life that you know you need to pay attention to but keep relegating to storage. The obvious things like mowing the lawn or preparing your tax return get done because they come with externally imposed deadlines. But the garage: we can simply keep the door shut and hope nobody notices.

One example of a garage in my life is the voluminous files from all my years in business that have absolutely no connection with what is going on today. I think about them often and I really ought to make time to get rid of them. Awhile ago, in getting ready for a major move, I'm sure I threw away at least a hundred files. Didn't make a dent. The remainder of the files still sit, waiting on me to make an irrevocable decision to "clean the garage."

I could give you many other examples, but my guess is that you have enough of your own without any help from me.

So why should you clean the garages in your life? Because having cleaned the garage is an absolute delight. You'll love the way it looks. And your spouse will love the way it looks, especially after you point out what a great job you've done.

I believe it was Gauguin who said, "I really don't like to paint. I just love having painted." Sounds like a garage deal to me.

I wonder if Michelangelo ever balked at taking the first chisel cut out of a big block of marble? Regardless of whether he procrastinated or not, I'm certain he knew that the tremendous effort, the hours of tedious cutting without much obvious result, was going to be worth it. And, I'm sure he loved having accomplished the task. So will you.

I can't tell you what will spur you on to tackle the garages in your life, but I can tell you that when you do take on the task, you'll find that the reward is *always* greater than the effort.

Spiritual wealth
has on its bottom line
one thing — love.

— Bill O'Hearn

Chapter 20

Accumulate Spiritual Wealth

What a different world this would be if only we had spiritual drive to match the gusto with which we pursue material wealth. If every person in the world were on a spiritual path, the hunger, the poverty, the greed and crime on this planet would disappear. I'm not talking about some type of socialism. I am talking about people leading from the heart for the greatest good of all.

I am also not suggesting that acquiring material wealth is wrong. But if we balance our spiritual quest along with our financial quest, things are better for everyone.

Have you ever known anyone who enjoyed tremendous financial success at the cost of their health, their family and their happiness? This is not uncommon.

I've known several, and I've never felt a moment of envy over their net worth statements. I pursued the almighty dollar myself for many years with so much vigor that there was not a lot of time or energy left to work on the rest of me. Again, it wasn't as though what I was doing wasn't right. After all, isn't the pursuit of financial freedom the American way? But the pace left me little time to assess the really important path in life.

I can't tell you precisely what happened to make me change. Maybe it was the cumulative weight of all my life's experiences, successes and failures, blessings and adversities. But whatever it was, I gradually listened to the wake-up call after pushing the snooze button most of my life. I began the study of the real Bill O'Hearn. I began to look around and ask some serious questions, like "What's this all about?"

I began to realize there is more to the universe than you can see when you wear blinders. I've always loved the outdoors, but even nature began to take on new meaning as I became more observant of the many blessings in my life.

Giving thanks for everything in my life became my common practice. Being aware of the needs of others became more habitual. Leading with love became more important. In other words, being a more spiritual being is an ongoing growth process in my life. As mentioned earlier, I've come to the conclusion that there is no final attainment of spiritual completion while on this earth — the practice of reaching upward and outward is why we are here.

I hope you will pause for a moment and assess how wealthy you are on your *spiritual* balance sheet. Maybe it is time to do a net worth statement of spiritual values rather than of dollars and material assets. If you decide to do this, I hope you will discover that you are already a millionaire.

But if not, take heart. At any given moment you can begin, and who knows? You might even find that in the search for your spiritual path, your financial path is enhanced.

*We sometimes forget that
all we really need
to be happy
is to have something
to be enthusiastic about.*

— Anonymous

Chapter 21

Live with Enthusiasm

There is nothing in the world more powerful than unbridled enthusiasm. Over the years I have enjoyed the enthusiasm of friends and acquaintances about many subjects: their jobs (although this is increasingly rare), their marriages, their faith, their health, their children, their avocations, their new car, new home, new anything — the list goes on and on.

But what stirs my spirit more than anything is experiencing and observing the enthusiasm about being fully alive, being enthusiastic for each moment of each day. There is something almost childlike in this kind of enthusiasm — a kind of heart that is open to the universe and whatever it has to offer — and maybe that is what draws me to it.

A couple of years ago I was reading an article in *The Oregonian* about Robert Lundberg, a lute-maker from Portland, Oregon. It described his passion for creating beautiful lutes. He told the reporter, "I am not working toward the perfection of my instruments. I'm working toward the perfection of myself."

I thought, *Wow! This is what it's all about!* I have always envied the artists of the world. They are blessed with the ability to participate in their passion. Shouldn't we all be so lucky?

But how do you bring enthusiasm into your life when there sometimes seems little to be enthusiastic about? Allow me to use an old adage, *Fake it till you make it.* Sounds kind of corny, doesn't it? But it works. Act as *if* — and it will *be*. I urge you to act as if enthusiasm for living is yours.

In the early days of my insurance career, I sought inspiration to go out and sell enormous amounts of life insurance. But I discovered a key principle, *perspiration precedes inspiration.* If I set my heart on a goal, with no holds barred, sooner or later I found myself with boundless enthusiasm for all that was happening. I discovered that the harder I worked, the luckier I got. And the luckier I got, the more enthusiasm I had.

Eventually I was able to relate the enthusiasm about my career and the principles I had learned to everything in life.

Being enthusiastic adds meaning to your existence. It adds meaning to the existence of others. I urge you to drop the veil of complication that surrounds your life and make a determination to live simply — and with enthusiasm. Then one day, sooner or later, you will awaken with an awareness that the world has become yours because of your *enthusiasm* — and your whole life will take on new meaning.

We have committed the Golden Rule to memory; let us now commit it to life.

— Edwin Markham

Chapter 22

Practice
the Golden Rule

Do unto others as you would have them do unto you.

It almost seems redundant to talk about the Golden Rule. The Golden Rule rests at the very foundation of all ten of the world's major religions. In the Christian world, it is stated as a commandment, "Love thy neighbor as thyself."

If the Golden Rule is so important in every major religion, why does it seem that so few people practice it on a full-time basis?

Maybe they don't believe it is important. Maybe they've never been treated in a way they would like to be treated and are simply returning the favor. Or perhaps an even bigger maybe — maybe they have never treated themselves as they would like others to treat them. I'm sure we could come up with all kinds of reasons, but that is not the purpose of this chapter.

My purpose here is to urge you to take a look at your practice of the Golden Rule. Is there a way that you can make it even more a part of your everyday life? Goodness knows there are enough opportunities for practice in any given day.

I believe one reason most of us do not practice the Golden Rule, is that much of the time we are in a reactive mode rather than a proactive mode. Here is an incident, which, without proactive thinking, could have caused a lot of stress.

Mary Manin Morrissey, who recently was honored by being invited to speak at the United Nations, tells this story about herself.

She had committed herself to practice the Golden Rule on a daily basis and was deter-mined not to react to potentially stressful situa-tions. As it turned out, shortly after Mary made this commitment, she was on her way to another state to speak to more than a thousand people. When she arrived by air, she discovered that part of her luggage had been sent somewhere else. The challenge was that all of her speech material was in the missing bag — and she never spoke without notes.

As she checked and rechecked with the young woman at the baggage claim desk, Mary felt herself becoming very upset. Even though it wasn't the baggage clerk's fault, it would have been easy for Mary to make her the object of her ire. Fortunately for everyone, before the fireworks started, she made a decision based upon her recent commitment and she began to treat the baggage clerk as she herself would want to be treated in a similar situation.

The important part of this drama began to unfold. Mary mentally stepped outside of the circumstance and asked the universe what the lesson was that was waiting for her to learn. She decided that maybe she was to talk to this huge crowd straight from her heart as always, but without notes — something she would never have done, unless forced to by circumstances. The result? The talk was a great success.

What about you? The Golden Rule starts at home. Are you willing to make a commitment to start treating yourself the way you would like others to treat you, so that you can go to the next level? Your life will be blessed if you do — as will the lives of those fortunate enough to experience the results of your new resolve.

Don't waste
a dollar's worth of energy
on a ten-cent task.

— Robert Eliot, M.D.

Chapter 23

Stay Loose

With the rapid pace of living today, it is easy to be anything but loose. We get pushed from all sides to be there and do that, right now. In the process of the push, our tension becomes tighter and tighter.

Look around and you will discover examples of people who get their buttons pushed on a daily basis. They are not the exception — they are the rule.

So let me tell you about a friend of mine, Lyle Nelson, who not only believes in the value of staying loose, but who is also a practitioner of that on a day-to-day basis.

Lyle went to West Point, where he learned some of the skills that would take him to eight U.S. Biathlon Championships and participation in four Olympic games. At the 1988 Winter Olympic Games in Calgary,

Lyle was unanimously elected captain of the U.S. team, and carried the Stars and Stripes in the opening ceremonies.

During his athletic career, Lyle learned the importance of staying loose, and witnessed many events in which superb athletes became uptight and allowed their tension to keep them from performing at their highest level.

You may have experienced, at some time or other, tension in your personal or professional life that kept you from performing at your best. If you happen to be a golfer, you've had the experience of missing a "knee knocker," a relatively easy three-foot putt you could make all day long — until there was money on it.

I can still vividly recall playing in a golf tournament (I believe it was my one and only Oregon Open appearance) many years ago in which I didn't just three-putt, I four-putted, from less than six feet. And when I missed that third putt, can you imagine how far that short little one-foot fourth putt seemed?

If, in a sport like golf, you can experience tension that makes you miss the easy ones, think about what happens in the rest of life.

Lyle carried his championship mentality over into his personal and business life. I have never observed Lyle in any other mood than happy. He may have his moments, but he has a stay-loose mentality about life in general. That mind-set makes it easy for him to be in a good mood regardless of what he is doing. And that good mood enhances his life and the lives of those around him.

The point I want to make to you is this: If it is true that staying loose is vital for athletes vying for championships, then it only makes sense that the same perspective must hold true in the bigger game. If you will develop a stay-loose mentality about all the circumstances of your life, you will increase your happy factor by many points and diminish your frustration factor immensely.

The next time someone or something attempts to push your buttons, whether it is in traffic, at work, or even at home, pretend you've made a New Year's resolution that you are bound and determined to keep. A New Year's resolution that simply says: *Stay loose!*

*We are born
into the world of nature;
our second birth
is into the world of spirit.*

— Bhagavad-Gita

Chapter 24

Take Your Spirit to Work

How do you take your spirit to work? Let's start by identifying what I mean by spirit. I looked up Webster's definition, but it didn't satisfy me, so I'm offering my own version. Your spirit is the God-given you, the inner you, your childlike heart filled with awe, energy, enthusiasm, excitement, anticipation and curiosity. Your spirit is the doer of good deeds, the giver of unconditional love, the part of you that cares and nurtures.

If you took your spirit, as I've described it, to your workplace, and started acting out that definition, would your coworkers think that you had flipped? Maybe. Yet how important is it that you do so? In my estimation, it is a matter of life and death.

I can hear you now, "Come on, give me a break. How could it possibly be a matter of life or death?" Consider this: Only when you are truly living from your spirit are you truly alive. And the only alternative — the opposite of being fully alive — is to be gradually dying.

Look at the workplace today. Is it a nurturing, caring, warm place to spend time? Generally not — but thank God for the exceptions. Recent surveys indicate that as many as 85 percent of Americans are not happy in their jobs. Could it be they are worried about making a living and don't have time to concentrate on making a life? If you consider that most people work eight hours a day and sleep eight hours a night, then they spend two-thirds of their lives either unhappy or unconscious. What are the odds that the remaining eight hours each day are filled with great joy and happiness? These grim statistics bring meaning to the words, "gradually dying."

What would it be like to go to work if everyone cared for each other, and there was abundant laughter and happiness? You'd probably think you had died and gone to heaven.

Is it possible to find a workplace like that? If not, it will have to start with you, at your workplace.

I had the good fortune to be my own boss for the majority of my career, which allowed me to control the atmosphere of my workplace by my attitudes.

My oldest daughter, Molly, was my right hand in the insurance business for several years. Our office was a fun, lighthearted place for both of us, which kept everything upbeat and positive. Because of that I was able to project this feeling out to my prospects and clients. It made for a great life.

But what if you work for someone else and have many coworkers? Can you take your spirit to work? Absolutely yes! And as you share your spirit, an unusual thing will happen. Remember the saying, "What goes around comes around?" Well, sooner or later you are going to be the beneficiary of the love, the laughter, the caring that you share from within.

It is a law of the universe. It is called the Law of Radiation and Attraction: Whatever you radiate you attract back to you. A magnet radiates its energy and metal is attracted to it. You can become a human magnet radiating spirit, and others with spirit will be attracted to you. Try it — it can change your world and the world of those around you.

I sought myself,
myself I could not see.
I sought my soul,
my soul eluded me.
I sought my brother,
and I found all three.

— Anonymous

Chapter 25

Be a Dirt Brother®

Jacques Nichols, a friend of mine, is a graduate of Stanford Law School and was an extremely successful venture capital guru who, in his own words, seemed to be partnered with Lady Luck. He had all the material evidence of success — a big home in a prestigious area, a country club membership, five late-model cars in the driveway, and one boat on a trailer and another at a permanent moorage on the Willamette River.

Then, in 1979, an unbelievable series of devastating events occurred. Jacques' two-year-old son died in January. In the spring, the infant daughter of his wife's niece died. Then another niece and her grandmother died in a plane crash on his birthday in May. His wife's aunt died in June and his mother died in October.

Financial troubles started to heap one upon another. Jacques contemplated ending it all.

A couple of his close buddies, who had troubles of their own, realized he needed a getaway and decided to take him fishing. On this fishing trip he had a revelation, which led to an awareness that the camaraderie they were experiencing was what life was all about. A flash of inspiration told him that they should call themselves Dirt Brothers. "Dirt," because of all they had been through, and "brothers" because that is what they were.

From that moment of inspiration in the boat, a movement called Dirt Brothers has evolved. Jacques developed a Dirt Brothers motto, which now appears on golf caps, sweatshirts, T-shirts and other items. The motto is:

> ***Laugh Hard***
> ***Hang Tough***
> ***Lend a Hand*®**

In reflecting on the Dirt Brothers motto, I came to the conclusion that the advice was solid and that I would devote the next three chapters to this message — a message that, by the way, has caught on with many professional golfers on the tour.

*Laughter is
dessert for the soul.*

— Bill O'Hearn

Chapter 26

Laugh Hard

Several years ago, Norman Cousins, author of *Anatomy of an Illness,* suffered from a rare disease called ankylosing spondylitis which causes the connective tissue in the joints and in the spine to disintegrate. The specialist working on his case said that the odds of recovery were about one in five hundred, and that he had never personally seen a patient recover.

Cousins had read someplace that negative emotions could create negative body chemistry; he wondered if positive emotions could create benevolent chemistry. He reasoned that if it could, then love, hope, faith, laughter, confidence, and the will to live had therapeutic value.

He decided to watch old comedians such as Laurel and Hardy, the Keystone Cops and the Marx Brothers.

Cousins discovered that even after a laughing session of only ten minutes, his infection rate would drop about ten points in the next two hours. Eventually he won the battle and was cured. He stated, "Evidence that attitudes could affect the course of my illness was a powerful regenerator."

Since that time, it has become more accepted in the medical community, as mentioned in an earlier chapter, that positive emotions have a positive effect on the body's chemistry.

How do you begin to bring those positive, healthy, emotions into your life? First, it seems that you have to continue to develop your sense of humor — to see the funny side of things and events that surround your day. You even need to learn to laugh at yourself. If that proves to be too tough, what would be difficult about renting an old comedy now and then — something with no real plot, but with the power to tickle your funny bone?

Wouldn't it be interesting if you put humor into your life on a regular basis, and in so doing your immune system is strengthened — and your resistance to things like colds and the flu increases dramatically.

Laugh hard — stay healthy. What a gift to yourself and everyone around you.

*Every challenge
contains the gift
of a greater knowing.*

— Anonymous

Chapter 27

Hang Tough

Hang tough. Think of all the songs that have been written about the tough times. Some of them talk about *how* to hang tough. One of the best in my memory was a song sung by Johnny Mercer, called "Ac-cent-tchu-ate the Positive." Here are some of the lyrics:

You've got to AC-CENT-TCHU-ATE the positive
E-li-minate the negative
Latch on to the affirmative
Don't mess with Mr. In-between
You've got to spread joy
Up to the maximum
Bring gloom down to the minimum
Have faith, or pandemonium
Li'ble to walk upon the scene.

What great advice. If we would only remember to accentuate the positive and eliminate the negative, a lot of our troubling times could be overcome.

I have never been in an adverse situation in my entire life, no matter how difficult, without being able to look around and see someone who has it worse. Remember the old saying that goes something like this: "I felt sorry for the man who had no shoes, until I met the man who had no feet." If we can stay aware that others have come through worse times, and can accept that there is a light at the end of the tunnel, we can be encouraged to hang on. Because times will change.

Dirt Brother Jacques Nichols certainly had more than his share of dark clouds in his life, but eventually he realized that he could bring the bounce back into his step in spite of circumstances. Even though he had experienced an unbelievable loss — loved ones, millions of dollars, house, cars and boats — he could still smile, because he had discovered something important. He had discovered that no matter how beat-up he was, he could still be upbeat. He knew there was someone out there who would reach down through the muck and offer him a hand — a Dirt Brother — and that made life worth living.

If you ever have less than positive circum-
stances in your life, *hang tough,* because there is
the spirit of a Dirt Brother out there, man or
woman, waiting for the opportunity to help.

*An effort made
for the happiness of others
lifts us above ourselves.*

— Lydia M. Child

Chapter 28

Lend a Hand

Sometimes all a person needs is for someone, anyone, to notice them. Yet it is easy for most of us to get so caught up in our own concerns that we are not aware of those whose path we cross. What does it mean to lend a hand? It starts with thinking of the other person instead of yourself, offering kindness without reservation, experiencing a true moment of selflessness.

The following story, described as an urban legend, was e-mailed to me recently. The tale, true or not, dramatically demonstrates the impact that a little kindness can have.

Stranded in the Rain
One night at 11:30 P.M., an older African-American woman was standing on the side of an Alabama highway enduring a lashing rainstorm.

*Her car had broken down and she
desperately needed a ride. Soaking wet,
she decided to flag down the next car.*

*A young white man stopped to help
her, something generally unheard of in
the conflict-filled 1960s.*

*The man took her to safety, helped
her get assistance and put her into a
taxicab. She seemed to be in a big hurry.
She wrote down his address, and thanked
him as the cab pulled away.*

*Seven days later a knock came on the
young man's front door. To his surprise,
a giant combination console color TV
and stereo record player was delivered
to his home. A special note was attached.
The note read:*

Dear Mr. James,

*Thank you so much for assisting me
on the highway the other night. The rain
had drenched not only my clothes but
also my spirits.*

*Then you came along. Because of
you, I was able to make it to my dying
husband's bedside just before he passed
away. God bless you for helping me and
unselfishly serving others.*

Sincerely,

Mrs. Nat King Cole

Maybe not all acts of kindness, or lending a hand, will have such dramatic results, but I can tell you without reservation that the more we lend a hand to others, the more others will be inspired to lend a hand. And the more people and situations that are positively affected, the better the world will be.

How about resolving to make it a daily habit to follow the Dirt Brothers motto —

Laugh Hard
Hang Tough
Lend a Hand

It is never too late to be what you might have been.

— George Eliot

Chapter 29

Choose a New Beginning

Every day, every hour, every minute, every second we are given a chance to start all over again. We are the only creatures on earth with this God-bestowed power, yet most of us do not comprehend this and continue to stay in situations or hold onto perspectives that do not serve us well.

Is it the human factor that keeps us stuck? I don't know, but I am certain it is not the spiritual factor keeping us in bondage. We all have unbelievable power within us, but something keeps most of us from accepting that truth. Maybe it is ego that thwarts our dreams by asking each of us, "Who do you think you are, anyway?" Whatever it is, let's go ahead and call the obstacle between mediocrity and glory "the human factor."

How do you bypass the human factor? I heard a story in church that might give an answer. It is a true story that was told to Ann Rothan, a friend of ours, by a well-known evangelist. Here is the story as I recall it:

> *When the evangelist was a young man, he was literally running from the law in an effort to stay out of prison. While police were pursuing him in his car, he spotted a big revival tent with all kinds of cars parked around it. He quickly ducked into the lot, and entered the tent. An evangelist was giving a hellfire-and-damnation sermon to a large crowd, and as the young man watched from the back, the minister suddenly stopped, looked directly at him and said, "Come up here, young man." He didn't know what to do, but anything was better than going back outside, so he went up on the platform. The preacher looked him in the eye and said, "There is more to you. It's time to repent — you are being called."*
>
> *At that moment, the young man felt an immense warmth come over him and he knew that he had been touched by the Holy Spirit, that he had been saved. He left the tent, turned himself in to the*

police, and went to prison. When he was released he entered ministerial training.

Years later, as he was traveling across the country in his ministry, he saw a little tent with the old evangelist's name on it. He had heard of the man's success, and also of his raging alcohol problem. He stopped the car, entered the tent, and introduced himself. After thanking him for showing him the light, he asked the minister a question. "There's something I've always wondered about. How could a known drunkard evangelize and save people? You are known as a falling-down drunk, yet people keep coming to you."

With that the old evangelist fell to his knees, grabbed the younger minister's ankles and said, "That is the miracle of miracles — that God would choose the lowest of the low to save souls."

Some people would say that the alcoholic evangelist had no business preaching and teaching the Word of the Lord, but I would not agree. Look what great work was done, not only through him but also through the young man. Literally thousands and thousands of lives were touched.

Well, so much for having to feel special or worthy to accomplish great things. We are all here as an important part of the universe. We are here for a purpose. And the more we are willing to risk going to the next level, the more we will serve that purpose.

So, remember that any day, any hour, any minute, any second you can take a deep breath and say, "That's it. *I'm choosing a new beginning* — starting right now!"

Believe it and go for it!

We do no great things —
only small things
with great love.

— Mother Teresa

Chapter 30

Make a Difference

.

Sooner or later, you will ask yourself "Am I making a difference?" Depending on your present age and experience, you may already have asked the question a hundred times, or you may not have given it a moment's thought. Yet! But trust me; someday the question will arise.

Is it possible for one individual to make a difference? Let me give you the short answer first. If you are awake and breathing, then you have at least the opportunity to make a difference. And that is as good a place to start as any.

The way you make a difference in this world is simply by being the real you, by revealing the beautiful diamond that is the center of your core.

You were born to be on purpose. You were born to make a difference. First, to your parents and family, then to friends and acquaintances, and eventually to strangers.

A poem by Thomas Dekker, who lived from 1570 to 1632, creates a word picture about making a difference.

The Life of a Happy Man

To waken each morn with a smile brightening my face;

to greet the day with reverence for the opportunities it contains;

to approach my work with a clear mind

and to hold ever before me, even in the doing of little things,

the ultimate purpose to which I am working;

to meet men and women with laughter on my lips and love in my heart;

to be gentle, kind and courteous through all the hours;

to approach nightfall with the weariness that brings sleep,

and the joy that comes from work well done.

This is how I wish to use wisely my earthly days.

Do you think that living the way Thomas Dekker describes would make a difference in your world? Especially if you go about it with *laughter on your lips and love in your heart?*

You only have to reach out and make a difference in the life of one person to have a positive effect upon the universe. A single kind deed may be magnified a thousand times and affect the lives of more people than you can imagine.

If you ever wonder whether you are making a difference, think back — if you can remember smiling at someone with love in your heart, you *are* making a difference.

Someday,
after we have mastered
the winds, the waves,
the tide and gravity,
we shall harness for God
the energies of love.
Then, for the second time
in the history of the world,
man will have discovered
fire.

— Teilhard de Chardin

Chapter 31

Live Only Love

The purpose of this final chapter is to encourage you to raise yourself to a new level of awareness. A level where living only Love permeates your entire being. A level at which your light will shine brighter within, so that you may send that light out into the world around you.

When I say, "Live only Love," I mean Love with a capital L. Every kind of Love you can imagine: Spouse Love, children Love, nature Love, kitty Love, doggie Love, friend Love, work Love, universe Love, and the list goes on, until finally we get to the two big ones — self Love and Creator Love.

Is it possible for the likes of you and me to live only Love? I honestly don't know. I do know it is a good idea to try. It turns out that the answer isn't in the stars

— the answer lies within each one of us. Wouldn't it be a delight if we could, moment to moment, day after day, live in the light of the words and wisdom of the all the great teachers who have gone before us?

I feel certain that if we only listen to our human side, we'll never make it. However, if we listen to our spirit side, we have a chance.

One way to listen is first to ask. I composed the following prayer especially for you:

*May God grant me this day
the wisdom, the insight and the strength
to shine my light within and without
so that I may truly live only Love,
and thereby serve the purpose of my
being.*

May God bless your journey toward *Life More Abundant!*

About *Ron Heagy*

When Ron was a sixth-grader he attended summer camp. His disabled friend couldn't go with him because the camp had no facilities for disabled children. Since that time, Ron has had a dream of establishing a summer camp for children with disabilities.

That dream is about to come true. Ron has obtained thirty acres near Sweet Home, Oregon, and is in the process of raising money to create Camp Attitude. A donor has agreed to match the first $25,000 Ron raises. Camp Attitude will be one of approximately eight such camps in the United States. His goal is to have a Camp Attitude in every state.

If you feel moved by Ron's dream, give him a call or write him.

Ron Heagy
32326 Old Oak Road
Tangent, OR 97389

Phone: 541-924-1400
Fax: 541-924-0379

For more information, and a view of Ron's beautiful paintings, visit his Web site: www.goron.com

To order copies of
Bill O'Hearn's other books:

From the Heart of a Child: $11.95
From the Heart of a Lion: $11.95
The Heart of the Matter: $12.00
Shipping/Handling 1–2 books: $3.50
Each additional book: $1.00

Contact: **Entheos Publishing Company**
3429 N. W. McCready Drive
Bend, Oregon 97701

E-mail: bbohearn@teleport.com
Fax: 541-330-9609
Phone: 541-330-9608
Order: 1-800-537-9991

To order additional copies of

Life More Abundant

Book: $12.00   Shipping/Handling: $3.50

Contact: **BookPartners, Inc.**
P.O. Box 922
Wilsonville, OR 97070

E-mail: bpbooks@teleport.com
Fax: 503-682-8684
Phone: 503-682-9821
Order: 1-800-895-7323

Visit our Web site at:
www.bookpartners.com